THE Amazing ADVENTURES of DALI BALLOONI

The Great

First published in Great Britain by Amazon UK in 2023

Text copyright © Dali Ballooni 2023
www.dali-ballooni.co.uk

Illustrations © Ilkhom Kasimov 2023

Editor: Louise Swann

ISBN 979-8-3786-6438-2

DALI BALLOONI THE GREAT IS A TRULY
FASCINATING CHARACTER AND THE FASTEST
BALLOON ARTIST IN THE WORLD!

He often gets into all sorts of adventures and some of them are described in this book. All of the stories are based on 100% true events.*

*According to Dali Ballooni.

Contents

INTRODUCING
DALI BALLOONI THE GREAT
A SAD BUT TRUE STORY ABOUT A MISSING PUPPY

Once upon a time, on a warm sunny day in London's Holland Park, a little girl suddenly began crying loudly. A man, who was passing by, stopped and politely asked what the matter was and if he could somehow help her.

However, instead of responding, the little girl suddenly paused crying and became completely distracted by the man's odd appearance. Not only was he wearing an extra tall top hat with an arrow through it and a pair of extremely long and pointy shoes but he was also carrying a quite oversized, old suitcase.

The tearful girl eventually explained, in a trembling voice, that she had lost her little puppy.

"Please don't shed any more tears," he said. "My name is Dali Ballooni the Great and I will help you! I have this suitcase full of modelling balloons which I can twist, with professional artistry, into any shape. I will make you a colourful puppy which will undoubtedly be even better than the one you had!"

Dali Ballooni promptly opened his suitcase, inflated several balloons and quickly made a beautiful balloon puppy.

He then proudly presented it to the little girl who hugged the colourful puppy affectionately.

However, just seconds later her face became sad and she started crying again.

"But I thought you liked my balloon puppy," said Dali Ballooni in great confusion.

"I do like it... but I still miss my other puppy. This colourful balloon puppy makes me realise how much I miss my little doggy. I think my heart is forever broken!"

"Oh, what have I done!" cried Dali Ballooni, kneeling right in front of the baffled little girl. "Will you ever forgive me?" he begged her, clasping his hands together.

A moment later, he suddenly brightened up, as if an idea had come into his mind.

"Actually, I can help you!" exclaimed Dali Ballooni confidently. With a beam on his, face he adjusted his bow tie and then enquired, "Tell me, when did you feed your puppy last time?"

"Around midday," she responded thoughtfully.

"So, that was over three hours ago... Well, that's it! Your puppy probably got hungry and then ran away, trying to find food of some sort. What's your puppy's name?"

"I call her Crazy... because she is always all over the place running, playing and chasing her tail!" responded the girl with a smile.

"I think I know how I can find her!" cried Dali Ballooni triumphantly.

Dali Ballooni then took a white balloon from his suitcase, inflated it and then twisted it into the shape of a bone.

"I'll be back soon!" he exclaimed and then started running all over the park holding the balloon bone above his head and loudly calling for the puppy.

"Crazy! Crazy! Crazy!" he yelled.

People in the park became quite concerned when they saw a man running around in a pair of very long, pointy shoes and wearing a very tall top hat with an arrow through it.

What made the scene even more alarming was that the man was holding a large bone right above his head and constantly shouting "CRAZY! CRAZY! CRAZY!".

Suddenly, from one of the bushes nearby, a cute puppy jumped out and ran towards him.

"Are you Crazy?" Dali Ballooni asked the puppy. However, instead of responding the puppy started chasing its tail. "Indeed, you are!" he observed, smiling.

Dali Ballooni took the puppy and quickly returned to the little girl.

"I am back and so is your little puppy!" he cried jubilantly.

"Thank you so much!" she responded with appreciation. "Can I also keep the balloon puppy that you made for me, please?"

"Of course you can. But do not forget to feed it or else it will run away too!"

"I promise I won't!" she said with a giggle "Dali Ballooni, you are truly the greatest!"

"Of course I am," responded Dali Ballooni proudly with his nose up in the air. "Well, it is really time for me to go. I have to get to the Moon as soon as possible!"

"To the Moon?" asked the girl with confusion.

However, by then Dali Ballooni was already far enough not to hear the little girl's question.

Indeed, the only time he turned back was when he heard a loud pop - Crazy had bitten the bone only to realise that it was a balloon!

The End

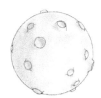

A PRESENT FOR THE KING

AN UNBELIEVABLE BUT TRUE STORY
ABOUT A SPECIAL PRESENT FOR THE KING

On one warm summer day, Dali Ballooni was making balloons for children playing near Buckingham Palace, which is in the very heart of London.

Unexpectedly, a well-dressed gentleman joined the line of children waiting for a balloon. When he reached his turn he formally introduced himself.

"My name is George The Royal Butler and I am here to ask you, on behalf of His Majesty The King, to make a present for him. His Majesty saw you making balloon sculptures for the children from one of the palace's windows and really would love to get one of your balloon creations."

"Of course!" responded Dali Ballooni adjusting his bow tie "but what balloon shall I make?"

"I am afraid His Majesty was rather vague... he just asked for *"a balloon present."*

"I see... please give me a second!"

Dali Ballooni quickly took several balloons and twisted them into the shape of a present box with a balloon bow on top of it.

"Here it is!" said Dali Ballooni excitedly, passing the balloon present on to the Royal Butler who looked slightly confused.

"Thank you very much. However, I believe that when His Majesty asked for a present, he was requesting a surprise, rather than the balloons shaped as an actual present box with a balloon bow on top." explained the Royal Butler as tactfully as he could. "You see, His Majesty will not be able to "open" your balloon present and will most probably get upset as a result..."

"You're right! I completely forgot to give you something else."

Dali Ballooni dug deep into one of his pockets and got out a small box.

"Inside this tin box, there is a special key which will allow His Majesty to open the balloon present without any problem - all he needs to do is just touch the balloon present with the tip of the key."

The Royal Butler took the tin box, opened the lid and then froze in confusion.

"Good gracious! This is not a key, this is more of a needle! If His Majesty touches his balloon present with the tip of this sharp key, then it will pop and scare him!"

"I am sorry to inform you that the only way to open the present is to use this very key. Trust me, everything will be just fine!" responded Dali Ballooni confidently.

The Royal Butler just shrugged his shoulders in bewilderment, thanked Dali Ballooni and then returned to the palace.

Minutes later, a loud pop was heard from one of the open windows of Buckingham Palace, followed by a short, but quite an audible yell from His Majesty the King.

Shortly after, a group of Royal Guards came marching out from the palace.

When Dali Ballooni realised that they were marching towards him, he was completely lost in a state of panic.

"Oh no! Oh, what have I done! Please do not chop my head off, please!" he begged the Royal Guards, clasping his hands together.

"Stop this nonsense immediately!" ordered their captain. "We are here to simply escort you to the palace. His Majesty The King would love to meet you in person."

That was a big relief for Dali Ballooni, so with a big smile on his face he took his suitcase and followed the Royal Guards. He was taken to the hall where His Majesty was sitting on a large, impressively decorated, golden throne.

"Hello Your Majesty, my name is Dali Ballooni The Great!" said Dali as he bowed courteously. "I hope that you liked the balloon present that I made for you earlier. I heard you open it."

The King was looking at Dali Ballooni with a serious face but then suddenly smiled.

"I should admit that your present was somewhat extravagant but, surprisingly, I have enjoyed "opening" it. It was both a very loud and satisfying experience - it made my day! The reason I have invited you to come to the palace is to kindly ask you to make as many of such "presents" as is humanly possible. I really would love to "open" them all!" said His Majesty excitedly.

"Of course. Your wish is my command!"

Dali Ballooni opened his suitcase, took out a lot of balloons and then instantly made hundreds of present-shaped balloons.

In no time, His Majesty's golden throne was surrounded by hundreds of such "presents".

The King did not waste any time and started "opening" the presents, one by one, with his sharp key. He was clearly enjoying the experience as every pop made him giggle like a little child.

It should be noted that His Majesty's servants and advisors who were present at the time did not find the experience as satisfying at all. Most of them were rolling their eyes and plugging their ears.

Before ceasing to make "presents" for His Majesty, Dali Ballooni took out some more balloons and made one last "present". It was extremely large in size.

"Your Majesty, please accept this very exceptional gigantic balloon present I have made especially for you."

"That's so very kind of you! Dali Ballooni, you are truly the greatest!" exclaimed the King, his eyes shining with delight.

"Of course I am," responded Dali Ballooni proudly with his nose up in the air. "Well, it is really time for me to go. I have to get to the Moon as soon as possible!"

"To the Moon?" repeated His Majesty with surprise.

However, by then Dali Ballooni was already far enough not to hear the question.

Indeed, the only time he turned back was when he heard an extremely loud bang: it was His Majesty enjoying the opening of his extra special, gigantic, balloon present!

The End

IN PURSUIT OF HAPPINESS
A HEARTBREAKINGLY TRUE STORY
ABOUT A MAN WHO LOST PURPOSE IN LIFE

On one gloomy day, Dali Ballooni went to Hamleys Toy Store on Regent Street to buy some modelling balloons and was saddened to see a miserable-looking man begging near the shop's entrance.

After a slight hesitation, Dali Ballooni approached him.

"Hello, my name is Dali Ballooni the Great and I am the most spectacular balloon artist in the world. I can see clearly that you are sad... and I wonder if you would allow me to twist a colourful balloon sculpture to brighten you up?"

The miserable-looking man shook his head.

"I am homeless, I have no family, no money, no luck... and, worst of all, I have no purpose in life to fulfil me. Thanks for the offer, pal, but your balloons won't help me."

Dali Ballooni only sighed heavily and then looked up dramatically, up into the air.

"Oh, what have I done to deserve this?" he exclaimed with passion, clasping his hands together and kneeling right in front of the miserable-looking man. "Why, oh why don't people appreciate the true power of balloons?"

Suddenly, Dali Ballooni's face brightened up and he addressed the miserable man with persuasion:

"Look, the balloon I would like to make for you will completely change your life! I will not accept no for an answer and will pester you until you agree to accept my offer!"

"Ok, ok..." responded the miserable man with a long sigh "...just get on with it and then leave me in peace!"

Dali Ballooni promptly opened his suitcase, took several balloons and twisted them into an unusual shape.

"Ta-da! Here it is - an extraordinary balloon backpack, which you must wear on your shoulders, allowing a balloon star to dangle over your shoulders and which you must repeatedly try to catch. When you catch it, you will find a purpose in your life!"

"That's easy peasy lemon squeezy." responded the miserable man "I will do so right now so you will just leave me alone."

The man put the backpack on and tried to catch the star dangling in front of him. However, it turned out to be a much harder task than he initially anticipated.

The miserable man continued in his attempts to no avail. He gradually moved forward a step each time he attempted to catch the star. At some point, he started chasing it until he completely disappeared from view somewhere around Piccadilly Circus.

One Year Later

On one sunny day, Dali Ballooni went to Hamleys Toy Store on Regent Street to buy some more modelling balloons. After the shopping was done, he was about to head home when suddenly he heard someone behind him calling his name.

When Dali Ballooni turned around he saw the miserable man whom he had met at the same spot twelve months earlier.

The man was wearing the same balloon backpack but surprisingly he no longer looked miserable at all! Indeed, he looked very happy, holding his arm around a beautiful lady standing next to him. The lady also looked joyful holding a newborn baby in her arms.

"Dali Ballooni, we are here to thank you VERY MUCH for the balloon backpack you made for me one year ago!" exclaimed the man joyfully.

"Back then, when I started chasing the balloon star attempting to catch it, I slowly moved forwards from one street to the next, from one city to another, from one country to another and then from one continent to another!"

"I travelled around the world trying to catch the star and I must admit it was an impossible task! As a matter of fact, I have never actually managed to catch it. However, along the way, I have met my soul mate who has joined me in my pursuits and now we have a family together! This is our cheeky little baby.

"Over these months, while trying to catch the star, I have visited many countries and eventually, I found a job as a travel author. I now write guide books for tourists! I have never been happier in my life! And all thanks are to you and your balloon backpack!"

Certainly, Dali Ballooni could see that the man, his wife and the little baby were all glowing with happiness.

"Dali Ballooni, you are truly the greatest!" suddenly they all said aloud.

"Of course I am," responded Dali Ballooni proudly with his nose up in the air. "Well, it is really time for me to go. I have to get to the Moon as soon as possible!"

"To the Moon?" repeated the man and his wife while the baby looked puzzled.

However, by then Dali Ballooni was already far enough not to hear their question.

Indeed, the only time he turned back was when he heard the baby giggling happily while attempting to catch the balloon star dangling above her!

The End

THE TIME MACHINE
AN UNBELIEVABLE YET TRUE STORY ABOUT TRAVELLING IN TIME

On a warm sunny day, Dali Ballooni was making balloon animals for children in Richmond Park when one of the children became curious as to why there was an arrow through Dali Ballooni's top hat.

"Well, it is a long story... you see, it's the pirates' fault," responded Dali Ballooni mysteriously.

"The pirates'?" the children exclaimed in disbelief.

"Yes, the pirates! You see, several years ago I invented the first TIME TRAVEL MACHINE completely made of balloons. I wanted to test it to make sure it worked. So, I took the decision to travel to a random point in time. It nearly ended badly, though; when I arrived at the destination, I saw some dangerous-looking pirates who instantly took notice of me and began surrounding me. The presence of pirates made me realise at once, that I was in the past!"

"In the past?" repeated children in awe.

"Yes, in the past, believe it or not! All of a sudden, one of the pirates pointed at my long shoes and then shouted (in a spine-chilling voice) that I was a monster of some sort. They instantly took out their

weapons and started chasing me angrily. Some of them were shooting bows and sadly one of the arrows pierced straight through my top hat."

Dali Ballooni shook his head with sorrow and then continued:

"And that's exactly how there came to be an arrow through my top hat. After having escaped from the pirates, I attempted to remove it but to no avail. So now I have no choice but to wear my favourite top hat with an arrow through it!"

One of the children's mother, who was standing nearby, overheard Dali Ballooni's story and then felt obliged to step into the conversation.

"Children, obviously, this man has just told you a fairy tale. As a responsible adult, I must advise you not to take it seriously," she said with importance.

"Oh, no, it was not a fairy tale!" objected Dali Ballooni adjusting his bow tie. "Of course everything I have just said actually happened!"

"Of course it DID NOT!" contradicted the lady with authority.

"Well, even though making a balloon time travel machine is extremely technical, I have no choice but to prove my words by making another one right here and right now!" continued Dali Ballooni.

"Well, go on then!" she responded, crossing her arms as she sneered contemptuously.

Without any delay, Dali Ballooni took a lot of balloons and in no time made a massive structure.

"Here it is - the Time Travel Machine completely made of balloons!"

"It looks more like a large telephone booth!" commented the lady with a smirky smile "Children, this man is a bamboozler! He has no morals whatsoever!"

Dali Ballooni rolled his eyes and shook his head.

"You can try it for yourself," he said with a sigh. "Please get inside, set the time and then press the red balloon button. The time machine will instantly transfer you to any time point of your choice!"

The lady exhaled noisily and then to make her point walked with determined confidence straight into the time travel machine booth. She quickly set a random time and then pressed the red button.

Seconds later the woman chuckled loudly.

"Ha-ha, nothing has changed, has it? See children, I told you it's all fake!"

However, when the lady opened the door she froze completely from shock. She realised that outside it was a completely different place from that which she had left, one which was full of huge rocks and tall ancient trees.

She cautiously stepped out of the balloon time travel machine and looked around. She sharply pinched her bottom

and blinked her eyes several times, only to realise that it was NOT a dream.

"Children, where are you?" she shouted despairingly at the top of her voice.

However, the only response she got back was that of a loud roar behind her. When the lady turned around, she saw a huge dinosaur looking at her from a distance. The sight of a dinosaur made the lady scream in panic and then she started running in random, zigzag directions.

The sight of some strange creature running randomly made the dinosaur quite curious and it started chasing the lady with the intent to play with her. However, this only made the lady run even faster and it was glaringly obvious from the expression on her face that the whole experience, by all means, was NOT something that she was enjoying.

At that moment Dali Ballooni unexpectedly exited the time travel machine waving his arms at her.

"I have just travelled in time to save you! Run here as fast as you can!" he shouted at the top of his voice.

Fortunately, the lady turned out to be a fast runner and seconds later she dashed inside the Time Travel Machine booth, quickly shutting the door behind her.

"Back! I want to go back!" she screamed right into Dali Ballooni's face in a complete state of panic.

Dali Ballooni gently nodded, adjusted his bow tie and then quickly set the required time on the dashboard, before pressing the red balloon.

"Ta-da! We are back!" announced Dali Ballooni with a smile, just a second later.

"Are you sure?" asked the lady, her hands shaking.

"One hundred percent!"

Dali Ballooni opened the door and when the lady saw familiar Richmond Park, she gave a huge sigh of relief.

They both came out of the time travel machine to be instantly greeted by the children.

"Tell us! Tell us! Is it true or not?!" they demanded surrounding the lady for an answer.

"Children, I have indeed travelled in time. A dinosaur chased me, hoping to eat me alive but Dali Ballooni heroically saved my life! As a matter of fact, Dali Ballooni, I must admit, you are truly the greatest!" she said emotionally, with a tear in her eye.

"Of course I am." responded Dali Ballooni proudly with his nose up in the air "Well, it is really time for me to go. I have to get to the Moon as soon as possible!"

"To the Moon?" they all repeated with surprise.

However, by then Dali Ballooni was already far enough not to hear their question.

Indeed, the only time he turned back was when he heard the children scream loudly as a huge dinosaur burst roaring out of the time travelling machine!

The End

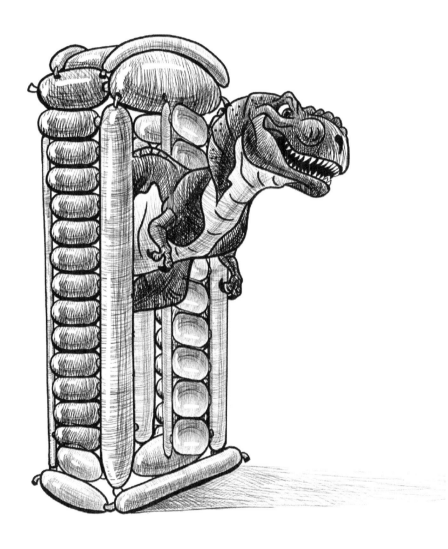

THE FAMILY AFFAIRS
A TRAGIC BUT TRUE STORY ABOUT FAMILY COMPLEXITIES

On a sunny day, Dali Ballooni was making balloons for children in London's Hyde Park.

At some point, a little girl approached Dali Ballooni and asked him to make her a golden princess tiara and a colourful princess wand. He instantly made both items and presented them with a smile. The happy girl thanked him and waved goodbye before running away.

Later that day, just before Dali Ballooni was about to head for home, an angry lady suddenly appeared out of nowhere.

"Your behaviour is unacceptable!" she exclaimed with an attitude.

Dali Ballooni was confused: he was not quite sure what she meant.

"You have made my daughter a balloon tiara and princess wand, and now she thinks that she is a REAL princess. She completely ignores my requests and says that she is not obliged to talk to *peasants* like me! I am consequently

under enormous pressure to deal with her "royal" behaviour and it is all your fault!" she exclaimed, pointing her finger right into Dali Ballooni's face.

"Oh, what have I done!" cried Dali Ballooni kneeling right in front of the angry lady. "Will you ever forgive me?" he begged her, clasping his hands together.

A moment later he suddenly brightened up, as if an idea had come into his head.

"Actually, I can help you!"

Without further explanation, he took several shiny balloons and quickly made a gorgeous queen's crown and a beautiful golden sceptre.

"I am going to make YOU into a QUEEN! Please put this crown on and hold your sceptre with confidence. Now, your princess daughter will not be able to ignore you: as no one can ignore a true QUEEN!"

Unexpectedly, the lady cheered up and gave Dali Ballooni a big, squeezy hug before merrily running away.

The following, day Dali Ballooni was making balloons for children at the same spot as before when out of the blue a man confronted him angrily.

"I will report you to the Police! Because of all your balloons my family life is now in ruins!"

"But what do you mean?" asked Dali Ballooni adjusting his bow tie and looking completely puzzled.

"Yesterday, you made a princess tiara and a wand for my daughter and she started behaving as if she was a real princess. You then made a queen's crown and sceptre for my wife and now she thinks she is a real queen. All I now hear are posh conversations and endless orders - do this, do that! I am fed up with it!!!"

"Oh, what have I done!" cried Dali Ballooni kneeling in front of the man. "Will you ever forgive me?" he begged, clasping his hands together.

A moment later, he suddenly brightened up, as if an idea had come into his head.

"Actually I can help you!"

Without further explanation he took several extra shiny balloons and quickly made an extra tall king's crown and a king's sword.

"I am going to make YOU into a KING! Please put this crown on and hold your sword with determination. Now, your princess daughter and queen wife will not be able to ignore you because no one can ignore a true KING!" said Dali Ballooni with the utmost courtesy.

The man's eyes shone with admiration and he gave Dali Ballooni a firm handshake before joyfully walking away.

Hours later, Dali Ballooni was still making balloons for occasional passersby when a sad, little boy approached him.

The boy looked miserable and when Dali Ballooni offered him a colourful balloon surprise, he just shook his head despairingly.

"No, I do not want your balloons. I have come to the sad conclusion that balloons only bring misery.

"You made a princess tiara and a princess wand for my sister and she started behaving as if she was a real princess.

"You then made a queen's crown and sceptre for my mum and now she thinks she is a real queen. On top of everything else, you made a king's crown and sword for my dad and now he thinks he is a real king!

"They all talk posh and give endless orders to me all day long, as if I am some sort of Cinderella. I am really tired of their constant demands and there's only you and your balloons to blame for."

"Oh, what have I done!" cried Dali Ballooni kneeling right in front of the little boy.

"Will you ever forgive me?" he begged the boy, clasping his hands together.

A moment later he suddenly brightened up, as if an idea had come into his head.

"Actually I can help you!"

Without further explanation, he took several blue and golden balloons and quickly made a wizard's hat and a magic wand with a shiny star on top.

"I am going to make YOU into a WIZARD! Please put this wizard's hat on and hold your magic wand with style. Now, your princess sister, queen mum and king dad will not be able to treat you as a servant anymore: no one messes with a true WIZARD - unless, they want to be turned into worms for a couple of days!" said Dali Ballooni and courteously bowed.

The boy's face was glowing with happiness and he gave Dali Ballooni a big hug before excitedly running away.

Later that day, Dali Ballooni was closing his suitcase to head home after a long day. Suddenly, he saw the familiar faces - the princess sister, queen mum, king dad and the little wizard brother - all wearing their balloons and looking very confident.

"Dali Ballooni, you are truly the greatest!" the little wizard boy suddenly exclaimed. However, the rest of his family shook their heads in disagreement, as they thought that THEY were the greatest.

"Of course I am," responded Dali Ballooni proudly with his nose up in the air. "Well, it is really time for me to go. I have to get to the Moon as soon as possible!"

"To the Moon?" repeated the whole family with surprise.

However, by then Dali Ballooni was already far enough not to hear their question.

Indeed, the only time he turned back was when he heard the magic wand's powerful swoosh and saw three little worms squirming around the little wizard boy!

The End

THE NEEDLEMAN
AN UNBELIEVABLE BUT TRUE STORY
OF DALI BALLOONI THE SUPERHERO

One day, Dali Ballooni was making balloon animals for children near Leicester Square's Odeon, when suddenly a smartly dressed man approached him.

"Hello Dali Ballooni, I am an extremely famous Hollywood film director and I would like to invite you to play the lead role in a new movie production. I think you will be perfect for the role!"

Dali Ballooni adjusted his bowtie and gave the film director the best Hollywood smile he could possibly produce.

"In order to make this offer extra special to you," continued the famous Hollywood film director, "you will be paid 10,000 balloons for each day of filming. Any particular colours and any shapes you'd like!"

"Amazing, I accept!" responded Dali Ballooni happily.

"Great! Then I look forward to seeing you tomorrow at this address." said the extremely famous film director, handing over his business card.

The following day, Dali Ballooni arrived at the film studio and was amazed to see the astonishingly realistic film set.

The extremely famous film director greeted Dali Ballooni and then explained what exactly was required.

"You will be playing the role of a balloon man superhero. We are about to start filming, so please come and stand here. The scene starts with you making a balloon animal for this little child."

The extremely famous film director quickly took his seat in the director's chair and shouted his instructions through a loud speaker.

"Silence on set, camera rolling and ACTION!"

At that moment, Dali Ballooni started making a balloon dog for the little boy waiting right in front of him. The boy clapped with excitement and happily took the balloon when it was done.

"Thank you very much Dali Ballooni! This is the best present I have ever had. You are truly the greatest!" exclaimed the little boy.

The boy was about to walk away when suddenly dark clouds completely covered the blue sky above and out of nowhere appeared a man who had no plan to conceal his dastardly intentions.

That man was wearing a long cape, a helmet with a huge needle attached to its top and a belt showing a large N on its buckle.

He unexpectedly popped the little boy's balloon with his needle helmet. The boy started crying bitterly and ran away to his mama.

"Ha-ha-ha-ha!" laughed the villain. "I will pop all the balloons in this world!"

Dali Ballooni looked completely shocked and with tears in his eyes he knelt holding hands together imploringly.

"Oh, why? Why did you pop the boy's balloon dog?" he begged for an answer.

"My name is the Needleman! I pop balloons because I do! Ha-Ha! No one will defeat me and I will conquer the WORLD!"

At that moment, Dali Ballooni quickly twisted a couple of balloons into a sword shape in order to attack the villain. However, the Needleman quickly popped it.

Dali Ballooni then made a balloon shield but it did not last even a second as the Needleman popped it too.

"Fear me, the Needleman super-villain! I will now pop you too, Dali Ballooni the Loser!"

The "loser" comment made Dali Ballooni so angry that while he was evading away from the Needleman,

jumping through obstacles, climbing on rooftops and leaping from one building to another, he suddenly came up with an amazing idea.

He quickly hid behind a large statue, took several balloons out of his pocket and made a large balloon magnet.

When Dali Ballooni jumped out of his hiding place holding a huge balloon magnet, the Needleman roared with evil laughter. However, by the time he realised that the magnet was attracting his metal needle helmet, it was already too late to escape. In just seconds the Needleman was completely stuck to the magnet by its powerful force.

"Please, please, let me go!" begged the Needleman unable to move. "I will stop being naughty! I will change my life!"

Dali Ballooni adjusted his bow tie and nodded his head.

"So be it; I will let you go but first you will need to apologise to the little boy whose balloon you popped with such careless cruelty," said Dali Ballooni pointing at the little child whose eyes were full of tears and who still held the pathetic deflated balloon poodle in his hands.

"I am sooo sorry!" sobbed the Needleman, weeping bitterly. "I was a lost man but I have changed!"

Dali Ballooni stood victoriously with his hands on his waist, in front of the defeated Needleman, looking far beyond the horizon to where the golden sun was setting.

"Cut! It's a wrap!" suddenly commanded the extremely famous film director. He looked exceptionally satisfied.

"Dali Ballooni, your acting was amazing and it only took us just one take to film the whole movie! Dali Ballooni, you are truly the greatest!" he announced into his loudspeaker and everybody on set, including the cleaner, started clapping their hands.

"Of course I am," responded Dali Ballooni proudly with his nose up in the air "Well, it is really time for me to go. I have to get to the Moon as soon as possible!"

"To the Moon?" repeated the extremely famous film director with surprise.

However, by then Dali Ballooni was already far enough not to hear the question.

Indeed, the only time he turned back was when he heard the extremely famous Hollywood director say into the loudspeaker:

"My next Oscar-winning movie will definitely be about Dali Ballooni's amazingness!"

The End

THE SPACE ODYSSEY
A HARD TO BELIEVE BUT TRUE STORY ABOUT A JOURNEY TO THE MOON

Once, Dali Ballooni was invited to a primary school to teach pupils and teachers how to make simple balloon animals. It was a lot of fun and everyone learned how to make a balloon snake, sword and flower. The children were extremely excited about their new skills.

"Dali Ballooni, you are truly the greatest!" exclaimed the whole class.

"Of course I am," responded Dali Ballooni proudly with his nose up in the air. "Well, it is really time for me to go. I have to get to the Moon as soon as possible!"

"To the Moon?" they all repeated with surprise. "Liar, liar, pants on fire!"

Dali Ballooni adjusted his bow tie and then self-importantly responded:

"Children, I am a grown-up and, as you all may well know, grown-ups never lie! I am going to the Moon TODAY!"

"Hooray!" shouted the children cheerfully.

Suddenly, the strict-looking headteacher, who was also present in the classroom, felt that she had no choice but to intervene.

"Children, I am very sorry to disappoint you but Dali Ballooni is simply joking. He cannot fly to the Moon!" she said with authority showing him a very critical look.

"As a matter of fact, Dali Ballooni, I must say clearly that it is NOT very nice of you to confuse these naive little children with your porky pie stories! This is a place of serious learning and I, for one, cannot condone such unjustified fantasies. Not only do you not have the appropriate training, but also lack a specialised flying device in order to undertake a trip to the Moon."

At that moment Dali Ballooni rolled his eyes, adjusted

his bow tie and then took a lot of balloons out of his suitcase and quickly made a balloon spaceship.

"Here it is!" exclaimed Dali Ballooni with his nose up in the air.

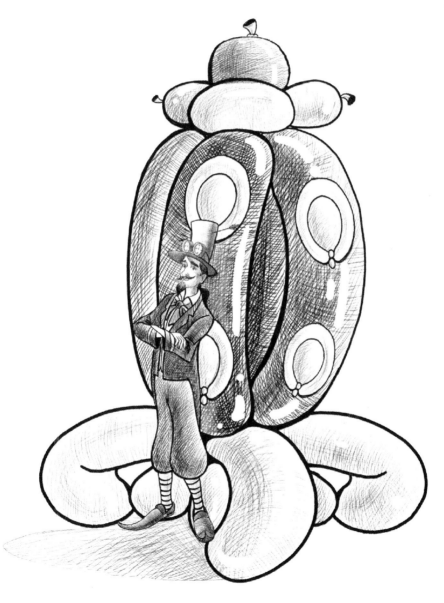

"There is it, indeed. However, your balloon spaceship simply will not fly: it has no fuel in it!" chuckled the science teacher.

"Further, the balloons will not resist the gravitational force value which is much greater than the lower limit of overpressure criterion, which will cause serious damage to the balloon spaceship!" noted the Maths teacher importantly.

Dali Ballooni just chuckled and rolled his eyes again.

"Well, of course, it does not have fuel in it. It does not need any.... as it flies using the POWER OF IMAGINATION!"

"The power of imagination?" repeated the Science and Maths teachers with great perplexity on their faces.

"Correct! Probably something you have never heard of!" commented Dali Ballooni with a cheeky smile.

"Dali Ballooni, why do you even have to go to the

Moon? Stay with us longer!" asked one of the children.

However, Dali Ballooni shook his head and responded with a solemn voice.

"I must get to the Moon as soon as possible in order to save a child who has accidentally arrived there because of my miscalculations."

All present in the classroom were looking at Dali Ballooni with bewildered faces, so he sighed and decided to tell the whole story.

THE SAD BUT TRUE STORY
ABOUT A GIRL WHO ACCIDENTALLY FOUND HERSELF ON THE MOON

(Narrated by Dali Ballooni himself)

On one warm but cloudy day, I was making some balloon animals for children at Piccadilly Circus in London.

Among the children waiting for a balloon, there was a little girl who dreamt of flying. So, when it was her turn to get a balloon, she asked me to make something that would give her the ability to fly.

Being a truly professional balloon artist, I quickly made a balloon jetpack with several very large round floating balloons attached to it. As soon as the little girl put the jetpack on, it started raising her towards the sky.

At first, all passers-by at Piccadilly Circus were delighted by the spectacle of the cute little girl floating above them. However, when a gust of wind suddenly pushed her further away from the ground, up towards the sky, people around understandably became very concerned.

At that moment, to my horror, the girl completely disappeared behind grey clouds. At that point there was already a huge crowd of onlookers, passers-by and tourists - all looking up at the sky anxiously.

I too was looking up until

an old man approached me and said with a trembling voice:

"You should be ashamed of yourself! The poor little girl is probably scared and lonely floating above the earth! It is all your fault! You are to blame for ALL OF THIS!"

"Oh, what have I done!" I started crying kneeling right in front of the old man. "How can I ever save her? Will she ever forgive me?"

A moment later, I suddenly brightened up, as an idea came into my head. I quickly dug deep into my pocket and

 took out a folding telescope. I carefully looked into the sky trying to locate the floating girl. Just minutes later I managed to locate her precise location.

"Dear onlookers, passers-by and tourists," I spoke loudly, so everyone who could hear me "I have just located the little girl in my telescope! The extraordinarily strong gust of wind has pushed the little girl far away from Earth towards the Moon. From what I can see in my telescope, she has safely landed on the Moon and is patiently waiting for help".

"It's all YOUR FAULT!" shouted that very old man, swinging his walking stick threateningly.

And indeed, it was my fault. I felt guilty and on the wrong side of the law. However, I knew that I could put it all right.

"I would like to assure you all that very soon I will personally travel to the Moon and bring the little girl back home!"

This message calmed everyone down and all onlookers, passers-by and tourists gave a sigh of relief and then continued minding their own business.

"So, children, this is exactly why I have to go to the Moon - to save the little girl!"

All of the children were captivated by Dali Ballooni's story and were sitting completely still until they heard once again the voice of the headteacher:

"Frankly speaking, I have not heard anything more absurd than this! Children, I must repeat myself, please do not take the words of Dali Ballooni seriously: as he is unsuccessfully trying his best to be a little bit funny".

Dali Ballooni rolled his eyes, adjusted his bow tie and then dug deep into his pocket to take out his folding telescope. He then pointed the telescope confidently towards the sky.

"Please, have a quick look," he asked the headteacher.

When the headteacher looked into the telescope, the expression on her face changed instantly. The telescope revealed the little girl standing on the Moon. She was holding a banner which read, "HELP!".

The headteacher turned towards the class and then said with a quiet and slightly broken voice:

"Children, I must apologise... Dali Ballooni was indeed telling the truth," she muttered, her cheeks blushing.

At that moment, all children started clapping their hands and whistling, so Dali Ballooni had no choice but to perform a courteous bow, with a huge smile beaming on his face.

"Well, children, it is really time for me to start my journey to the Moon!"

Dali Ballooni took the balloon spaceship that he had made and then went outside the school. On the school playground he took some more balloons out of his suitcase, tied them together to make a long line which he then attached to a couple of trees. Then, he stretched the balloon line as much as he could and loosely tied it to the ground.

"Goodbye children and grownups!" he shouted at the top of his voice, as he entered the spaceship.

"Goodbye Dali Ballooni The Great!" children shouted back.

"What a remarkable man!" said the headteacher wiping away the unexpected tears rolling down to the tip of her nose.

At that moment, the stretched rubber line released and catapulted the spaceship far into space. Dali Ballooni was looking down from the spaceship's round window and waving everyone goodbye.

The End

Will Dali Ballooni's mission succeed?

Will he meet any aliens on his way to the Moon?

Will he return back to the Earth safe and sound?

TO BE CONTINUED...

Printed in Great Britain
by Amazon

37621984R00051